On being "the bad guy":
Neuroqueer Self-Realizations
in the Algorithmic *Envirusment*

ISBN: 9781088281475

Published by Ingram Spark

Cover designed using Nightcafe & Canva

Printed in United States

First Edition

Table of Contents

Acknowledgements

To everyone continuing to wear a mask, in order to protect themselves and others from C19. And to all the autists who have isolated and masked in order to survive and live as who they are today.

Introduction.

Nothing made life clearer to me than COVID-19. I realized that I wasn't who I thought I was, and I had no idea who I was. So, it was easy for me to be over-drinking and -working. It's been four years, and I have hardly seen anyone in person. Because most people have decided that all of our lives don't matter. They have been led to ignore an ongoing cardiovascular disease, that, the more you get, the more likely it is to disable / kill you.

I really don't know what else to say about that. (Except, I guess, also, this whole fucking book.)

However ill-informed their ongoing denialism is, to them and us, this second volume of my memoir, just like the last, isn't to talk about them.

It's to talk about me. And to reveal how I learned, unfortunately, the sheer amount of people who, for most of their lives, didn't know that they were autistic changes Absolutely Fucking Everything.

Meanwhile, I know that there's also a fuck ton more people (sometimes overlapping into a Venn diagram) who have remained COVID conscious for the last four years and counting. Many of these folks are suffering from extreme isolation, loneliness, and life re-processing in an age, where

-- most everyone we've ever known -- now doesn't give a Single Fuck if we all live or die.

What is one supposed to do if they've just found out who they are during, seemingly, the end of the world…? Just like before, everything I say herein is not hyperbole. People treating colonial capitalist reality as hyperbole is why some of the country is now on fire and another part is floods.

We have plenty of research that shows colonial capitalism has -- quite literally -- been hurdling us towards the climate apocalypse. This is why I ended the first volume of this, stating that all very directly and clear. We literally don't have enough time to pretend as if that's not the fucking case. And I think it's time we respect autist directness as a Very Useful message for people to: get with the fucking program, so that more of us don't die.

In the United States, autists (formally Dx or not) have long been treated as if we are "too much" of everything. No matter how we act. No matter if we mask or not.

Contextually, in this late-stage neoliberal capitalist *envirusment* era, humans continue to act as media in society building processes. Meaning, in new algorithmic forms, they've successfully taken all things "natural" and commodified them, including intimate relationships. Nothing that exists is sacred anymore, for better and for worse.

So, what are we gonna do about it?

Just like the first volume. I have more puns, cusswords, and trauma than answers, but reading my back story in volume one will in fact be important for anyone who wants to understand the fullest perspective of my Dr. bird's eye view. So, it will be best understood if you read not just this volume, but also the first. In short, I live a life of a late in life realized autistic person who struggled with statistically-backed amounts of substance abuse in the sexually violent U.S. ecology. This book is about my *envirusment* life.

To make something crystal clear that I didn't mention in the first volume, recent research has shown that the vast majority of autists who do choose to self-diagnose are accurate in doing so.

So, what does this mean in the *envirusment* era?

Well....with what we know about how many autists are high likelihood for a Very Long list of comorbidities, we are at high risk for COVID-19.

As stated at the end of the first volume, we also know upwards of 80% of us who were assigned female at birth (AFAB), are not formally diagnosed by the age of 18 (if we ever get Dx).

There are countless lost generations of autists who may or may not ever learn that they actually are autistic. And perhaps most tragically, with eugenics and fascism returning, it's not safe to be openly autistic for any of us. But we are autistic all the same. Not having a formal diagnosis does not change the fact we experience(d) lives that are, more or less (uniquely experienced) yet often similar to, what a formally diagnosed autist does. That's what my first memoir details extensively.

And to be honest, it's ridiculous that I even need to say that. But too many people treat categories as if they are the marker of what reality is, when anyone who knows language, of course, knows that is not true. However, unfortunately, most of us are taught not to think about that. Like, we're not taught to think about -- almost everything -- that has happened and continues to go on to this day.

That's what makes this *envirusment* era unique.

Not only are we just now realizing what self-realizations -- en mass -- of autists mean about our brains and what is "normal". But we are also realizing -- in the same time period -- how common queernesses are. How fabricated the idea of "straightness" has always been. It's a rather new invention passed off as having existed forever as our default. We must always remain vigilant to language usage when talking norms.

There is no such thing as "straight" without any one culture's binary language, used to describe biological sex and/or gender. Hence why, within the first volume, I began by referring to Dr. Nick Walker's term "neuroqueer" in efforts to detail ways that neurotype and queernesses intersect.

Readers may also see works like *Spectrums: Autistic Trans People in Their Own Words* edited by Maxfield Sparrow, only a few years earlier. And/or, Dr. Devon Price's *Unmasking Autism*.

Anyhoo, point of me saying that is "Straightness" is just one option. To say otherwise is to ignore everything that's ever happened. And it's the same with gender. And and, it's the same with neurotype, etc. That's why neuroqueer self-realizations in the algorithmic *envirusment* changes -- quite literally -- Everything. They challenge dominant concepts of normal self-identity, relationships, and institutional legitimacy, opening doors to liberatory worlds.

When done appropriately, the three critical media ecological tenants I discussed in volume one: we only know we know, everything becomes normal in repetition, and everything is connected, reveal (often) totally new worlds within all our unique capacities to build. But, first, we have to look back at what has been. We have to look back at the Breakdowns that have led to Breakthroughs.

AND Boy, do we autists have a lotta fucking Breakdowns. So, there are also many Breakthroughs to be had. Mass neuroqueer self-realizations are just a coupla breakthroughs paired together. And, as countless artists, activists, and critical cultural scholars have said, for a — very *Very* long time — these characteristics (neurotype + queernesses) compound with every other demographic.

I don't know about y'all, but I don't want to live in a world where I have no hope for the future. I don't wanna live in a society where people pretend as if a thing that's killing us, isn't killing us, so that they can eat inside at Chili's.

Every single time I watch anything on a streaming service anymore, I'm reminded of how much people don't give a single fuck about anything besides money.

Whenever I go onto algorithmic platforms, all I see is people not being able to afford to live.

And I'm one of those people. Despite all of my student loan, debt and education, right now I can't afford to fucking live. And we all deserve better. So, without further fucking ado...........

This volume is about how we all deserve better than what I'm about to recount from my last four eye-opening, isolated, impoverished years. As to be expected, this second manuscript builds on my volume one in which I shared my early life (my first 30 years), to best contextualize how and why I've lived my last four, since COVID-19 hit.

Spoiler alert, my dear readers, it's been a deeply lonely, now almost, 5 years. I have never spent so much time alone in my entire life. I am somehow still alive. I'm not sure if I've caught COVID-19.

And there's a good chance I may never know.

Thus far, millions of people have died globally.

On national and global scales, we are also years into what researchers have called a loneliness epidemic. We are also years into the sex apocalypse, where people are having less sex. Fascism is returning. Most folks are ignoring both COVID-19 and the visibly worsening climate crisis (near daily new natural disasters). Meanwhile, I'm mostly inside my apartment alone. When I go out, I see people acting like none of this is happening. I can't even fathom it.

The last four years I have been stuck between a deep loneliness and inability to afford to live.

Nearly every day, I wake up to still exist within a U.S. society that wishes I (an autistic queer person) was dead. To many of them, I am a

neurotyped mistake. To most everyone autistic brains are a mistake. To many others, my body is also a mistake. But you know what?
This bigoted fucking society hasn't killed me yet.

So now, I'm a living speaking fucking problem it's absolutely going to have to fucking deal with.

In the first volume of my memoir, I talked about my life before March 2020. For sake of not repeating myself, this volume will discuss other details of my 2020, 2021, 2022 and 2023 years.

Occasionally, when relevant, I may make mention of things I already went over within the first volume (where, again, I talked about the first 30 years of my life, so readers can understand where exactly I'm coming from (because obvi, I'm a culmination of everything I've learned by living).

I only knew what I knew, everything became normal in repetition, and everything was connected to what I'm now experiencing daily.

That means going in chronological-ish order, each of these chapters is going to be categorized as follows: [Two-] Zero [-Two-Zero.], [Two-Zero-Two-] One, [Two-Zero-Two-] Two, and [Two-Zero-Two-] Three. This volume is much more concise than the first one because I'm only painting a brief picture of *who* and *how* I was

suffering the first 30 years of my life, became
who I know am, and exist as, during the last four.

In doing so, I comprehensively discuss the stark
differences between *how I lived then*, before
March 2020 and *how I lived the last four years*.

I did my best to viscerally unpack for everyone
exactly what it has meant for me to have had my
own personal self-realization in this *envirusment*.

Truth be told, this is what I expected my first
book to be. Then, I realized (while writing it) that
I actually needed to dig into my early life before I
could write this part. I needed to do that, both for
myself, but I also needed to do it, so that I could
write this second volume. Or else it wouldn't
have made anywhere near as much fucking sense
to most people who are about to read this one.

Therefore, my goal by the end of this volume is
for it to make better fucking sense as to: *why* I
feel so strongly about still being/care to be
COVID conscious in a world of folks who don't.
Maybe some of them do, but they don't *act* like
(take preventative measures anymore) they care.

Also, *why* I now can't imagine that. This is my
explanation as to *why* I can't imagine not caring,
after my miserable lifetime of mostly not giving a
fuck if I lived or died, as an unrecognized autist.

It's easy to not care if you live or die if/when you're not living as who you fucking are. This is the story of who I fucking am, and how I don't want to die now that I am. So..........Now, What?

Chapter [Two-] Zero [-Two-Zero.]

Welcome back to March 2020! It's *Absolutely Terrible* here. (For anyone that would like a more in-depth description of my 2020, I invite you to check out chapter 4 of the first volume of my memoir, that gives you all the bits and pieces that most people on the outside could already see. But if you **have** read it, or are just looking for more of that internal ushy-gushy mushy-mushy stuff, you've come to the right second volume place.)

Recently, I attended a Story Center workshop.

As told in chapter two of my first book, I survived being falsely imprisoned at 23-years-old. So, for this workshop, I chose to make a digital story about that horrific experience. Not for trauma porn, but to highlight to the public in my locale the statistics about how upwards of 80% of AFAB autists aren't diagnosed by 18, and how 9 out of 10 of us live #metoo lives anyway.

In my story, I included a clip of paint swirls. It was an abstract motion picture that looked like, and symbolized the feeling of how, once, when I was on a field trip to the Indiana Dunes as a kid, while trying to ride waves, my face hit the bottom of Lake Michigan, and my nose bled, profusely.

At 23, false imprisonment also blended my blues and greens, mixing them with the stark redness of my own blood. It was how weightless danger felt.

Sorry in advance, dear reader, but keep this all in mind, as you imagine that it's March 2020 again.

Imagine Swirling Breakdown(s)

Imagine you had been working on your PhD for two years full-time, before it happened. After a few months, imagine that the one faculty member who advocated for you, above anyone else, stepped down from your committee because you relied on them too much (which was true, and no hard feelings) and then a week later, your mom called to say she's about to die, and was being put on home hospice and **Loads** of morphine.

My memory of 2020 feels like eerie blue / green blurs, swirled with my warm blood from a hard impact, too. That first year of COVID-19, I was completely alone in an old moldy ass apartment.

The longer I stayed there, the more it – literally, not figuratively, made my nose bleed. Then, one day my landlord tore apart my front deck that had a cool bench, replacing it with a bad construction and paint job, shitty one, without any notification.

Imagine being four hours away from anyone you ever knew who'd harmed and/or supported you, grieving the loss of the person who brought you into this joyful and awful world, and not being allowed to see anyone besides behind a screen.

Then, imagine that your dad contracted COVID-19, only two days after your mom had just passed from lung cancer. And not being able to have or attend her wake until a month later, while you wait to see if your dad might, shortly, die too.

Imagine during all of this you are also deep in the major crunch time of completing your PhD program courses, after a full 2 1/2 years, where -- after each and every semester -- you had to re-teach yourself how to breathe (because you're an unrecognized autistic person and didn't know).

Imagine not being allowed to take a break by university administration, later that same month.

Can you imagine it? (Imagine: disassociation.)

Breakdown(s) from a Dr. bird's eye view

Before COVID-19 arrived, I had always thought I hated video calling. It felt **So Very** impersonal.

There weren't any eyes for me to connect with (in that way I'd learned my whole life to survive).

Anyway, I thought that (literal prolonged eye contact) was what I was supposed to be doing. Turns out, as an autist that I took eye contact *Far Too Literally*. (So typical of me -- an autist!)

In time, much like compulsory heterosexuality, I had learned to accept and embody the video call.

All my literal eye contact in person left and was replaced with only **Zoom**. After my first online MEA conference, I remember I still feeling the emptiness after logging off. It was new, then.

It reminded me of how, years before this, I'd described to a few people about a distinct awareness that I have had ever since I first moved from my childhood home into a new apartment.

The feeling I got after first moving in, knowing it didn't feel quite like home yet. Knowing that, eventually, that newness feeling, would disappear. Zoom worked exactly the same way.

In 2020, some people told me that I didn't grieve "the right way". I never wanted to talk about it out loud, using my actual voice. Just text. What was there for me to say? I was completing my PhD coursework, as a part of the most connected humanity during a pandemic that'd ever existed.

I remember attending Zoom panels where (pre-COVID graduated) alumni did their best to give advice for a job market that they had never experienced. The uncertainty of it all sickened, disabled, and profitably deadened our futures. It filled in infinite squares, Zoom squeezed us into.

People complained Zoom just wasn't the same. In the beginning, me included. But the longer Space happened, I learned that it's for better and worse.

A week before my mom had passed away, she finally disclosed to my older sister and I that she had, in fact, sued many companies for her lung cancer. She'd traded silence for blood money.

The many corporations that are responsible for poisoning my mom to death, filled her margaritas to stay silent and fed, inside of the same Mexican restaurant that my (dead to me) extended family members screamed racist shit at me at, a few years before she died from it, on home hospice.

I lived 2020 almost entirely inside my own head. Sometimes with my body, I took a lot of drives.

First, to get out of the house, once in a while. But also, to pick up some nice vegan food about 30 or 40 minutes away, just so that I would have somewhere to go with at least a KN95 mask on.

Many people were at least wearing a mask, then.

Even with all the horrors, it was a year most everyone, at least, still pretended that they gave a single fuck about anyone's life besides their own.

After my mom passed, I had more money than I could possibly know what to do with and had no where I could safely enjoy in public. That first year of living without third spaces, but with everything I could buy and more, was surreal.

For a couple years, I had been living without almost every basic thing I needed to survive inside a large 2BR / 2LR apartment, that was now making my nose bleed. Some friends sent me "Sorry your mom died during a global pandemic" flowers. Others wanted me to talk to them, but all I needed to do was be alone in the company of just my own silence. They just didn't understand.

That year, shortly after my mom had passed, I embraced the financial freedom to actually start paying for things that I had been living without. There is an entire mental process I was living. It was an unlearning process that "I didn't deserve anything I needed to exist". It took a long time.

It was an unmatchable, arduous, and unattainable, privilege most people will never experience, ever, let alone during such an incredibly traumatic time. I can certainly say that, without that, I wouldn't have survived. Not a chance in fucking hell. It's still didn't make it all better. Because, while money is freedom, it still doesn't make up for the profitable poisonous death of your mother.

Buy 2 Breakdowns, Get 2 Breakthroughs Free!

I paid off all my credit cards. The credit card companies didn't understand that, at first. First, they presumed that I'd maxed out all my cards.

So, they tanked my credit score. I, then, had to call them to tell them I paid them all off, and they fixed my credit score. That's how rare it is for a millennial to suddenly receive lots of money, to be released from their credit card debt. (And, yes, I didn't touch my student loans because fuck em.)

By the point I received this blood money, I had long lived the 90s episodic trope of spending far too much on credit cards and was now transitioning into the Rugrats "Chuckie Finster is rich" episode where his family won the lottery and they splurged. I had all kinds of fancy things delivered to me. None of them made me happy.

I bought real haircutting shears off of Amazon and learned how to cut my own bangs while I waited for all of the bleach blondeness to grow out from my roots into my natural brunette. It was very symbolic of the fact that, not only was I bleaching my hair, but I had been bleaching basically my entire sense of self to present a version of me to the world in a more non-autistic way. I needed to grow, and cut, *ALL* that shit out.

One of my favorite purchases ever was I bought a frame to hang my yoga swing on. During the summer before I started my PhD, I was gifted yoga silks by one of my Yoga friends. But, all that time, I could never hang them anywhere safely. So, I just didn't do anything with them until I could afford to buy this frame to hang them in my apartment. At that point in my PhD, I was barely doing the amount of headstands that I used to, and my yoga practice had basically dissolved. But that yoga swing allowed me to do inversions without the grounding I used to have. I was a bird in flight. And I posted it all over the Instagrams. Other times, I would just sit inside it.

(For anyone that doesn't know, this makes it basically just a sensory swing. When safe, I highly recommend feeling the weight of your body, cradled like a little baby, by some silks.)

I got a foot massager, and one of those massagers you drape over a seat for your high/low back and shoulders. I got Roombas that sweep your floors, and then mop up after (mostly the sweeping one [I named Gerald] just destroys everything in your home that gets in its way. That's so, Gerald!).

At some point, I finally requested that my shitty landlord fix the stripped wood spots on my floor.

After they did so, I breathed in poison for days from the varnish that their maintenance people covered all the patches of stripped wood planks in. And as someone who had, only newly learned, they're now 4 x as likely to die from lung cancer.

In the grieving meantime, I bought all the basic things average people wouldn't imagine living without. Blood money reminded me "oh ya, I'm a person too," a reminder most poor people never access (like the final boss stage of Scientology where you finally learn that Lord Xenu exists).

Except in my case, Lord Xenu was the COVID era existential crisis that corporate silent blood money didn't replace the death of my mom. (This is also why, a couple years later, I finally wrote Mother as Calendar, available on my SubStack.)

That first month of her passing, some kind folks delivered me care packages, or homemade meals.

A friend of mine, from my masters, sent me a very well-manicured witchy gift box, put together with care. My first tarot deck was inside. (They say the first one always needs to be gifted.) This one was in the style of gypsies. Very appropriate.

Occasionally, I would hang out on Zoom with some people from my PhD program. But, as I described in the first volume, I never really got along with them. I realized I only drank when I was on Zoom with them. Otherwise, when I was entirely by myself, I never felt the need or desire to drink. That was a miraculous realization, that took me a very long time, while grieving the loss of my mom and my entire outside life, to process.

As I described in my first book, I have drank heavily in public, almost my entire life. It was such an enormous part of my identity. I really thought that it was who I was, then. I thought that I was just an alcoholic. Even though, for all that time, I basically never had a drink at home by myself because I never enjoyed the feeling of it.

Yet, somehow, for 30 years, my never drinking alone never clicked for me, until COVID-19 hit.

After a while, with organizations explaining that we need to wear masks, I realized that it wasn't safe for me to continue going to a laundromat, or anywhere, during this scary global pandemic.

I remember realizing at one point in my early years of COVID, as I was preparing for my dissertation on sociosexual ecologies, that some people were going to fetishize wearing masks and not social distancing. And that it would definitely become a porn category soon. (People fetishize basically anything -- you can possibly imagine.)

And not to yuck anyone's Yum, but I knew that this one was going to be especially disappointing

to see. Because it was going to sexualize the act
of endangering all of our lives, and for profit.

Not too long after that, the CDC recommended
that people go to glory holes as a safer alternative
to being sexual, but behind a wall, to prevent
COVID. Obviously, that went in my dissertation.

I started getting all my groceries delivered. The
grocery store always overstimulated me anyway.
So, this was a welcome, although overpriced,
accommodation. I bought a couple of those small
washers and dryers for my apartment. And then I
realized, eventually, after months and months of
nosebleeds from being inside that huge moldy ass
apartment — apparently, far too much more —
than before, I needed to get the fuck outta there.

Can't Speak Into the Air? Down the Rabbit Hole

That, and my mom's lung cancer, plunged me
down a rabbit hole of learning about indoor air
quality. Spoiler alert: on average, it's *Absolutely
Terrible* thanks to colonial capitalism. I did a lot
of research about air quality. I learned a lot about
it, lead pipes, and how absolutely terrible they all
are. How much they're all killing us because
colonial capitalism poisons our loved ones to
death for profit, inside and outside of our homes.

And it does it silently without us even knowing it.

Because it's not responsible for the collective repercussions of material preservatives and other chemicals all over, basically, every product that's ever been manufactured. But those chemicals still collect in our air, all around us, inside our homes, killing us slowly. (And yes, just like that one song, because colonial capitalism is romanticized and fucking abusive.) Just like any predator, it will gaslight you out of believing what you know.

Most every U.S. institution will treat you like what you see with your own eyes isn't valid if their organization is behind you in seeing what you've connected. Especially if your pattern recognition is great. This world doesn't like you if your pattern recognition is great. It's hates you.

And you have to still keep living in it, anyway.

The key *envirusment* difference between this first year of COVID, and my early life, was: isolation.

But not only was I more physically isolated than I ever had been before, but I was more connected via platforms than I ever was before too. And, as anyone who studies ways that systems implement bread and circuses (giving the people what they need and then dividing them, so they can't talk) knows, *that's a difference that made a difference.*

The longer I was physically alone, with only algorithmic connections, all I had was time to grieve and think about my life. I had no idea how long this pandemic would go on at that point, but that first year got my mental ball *fucking rolling*.

That same year, I met someone on Twitter, who was a much-more-open-about-it autistic person. I messaged them to talk about my own realization.

They were Hella helpful to me. It was like I got an autism welcome basket. They told me about a poetry night that they were reading in soon. It was stationed out of New York, but on Zoom. I attended and met a bunch of cool and legit poets.

They had a poetry night every Monday night on Zoom, then. So, I started attended it regularly, and would sometimes talk with them afterwards.

Later on, I read some poems myself, and then, eventually, I was grateful to publish in their KGB Bar magazine (some COVID infatuation poems).

The remainder of this chapter is what I had only just begun to realize to myself during late 2020.

COVID-19 Autism Masking Breakthrough(s)

Late 2020 made me exceptionally aware that we (and all our bodies) are surfaces for COVID-19 in the *envirusment* era. I became painfully aware of every single thing's place in space I touched with my hands, especially, before I was about to eat.

To resolve this experiential existence crisis, after I would wash my hands, I designated my left hand as the one that I touched food with during eating. Whereas my right hand is the one that I can touch all else. So far, this has worked for me.

Before you judge me, my first-hand (literal) tediousness follows handwashing habits that health organizations suggest we follow, so we don't transmit COVID-19. (I also never went so far as to washed my groceries. So, let me do this).

And as far as I know, it's helped me make sure I don't get COVID. Alongside other regular handwashing habits, like after I touch anything I think might have gotten COVID on it. For better and for worse, the skin on my hands dealt with it.

But this wasn't the first time I was being hyper-attuned to my body in space. I'm an ol' pro at it!

Many non-autistic folks can't begin to understand the level of self-policing that I was undergoing for the first 30 years of my life, even when I was living entirely alone. That was the default way for me to exist: under constant vigilance / duress.

And I don't mean this like somebody who just lives with PTSD hyper-vigilance. Even though of course, yes, this certainly also interplays with my personal experience, as an autist that has had to pretend to be someone they're not my whole life.

What I mean is that I was basically existing as a manic pixie dream girl, 24/7, even when I was entirely alone, convincing myself that's who I was. Because I didn't know who I actually was, and I had to keep up that charade for everyone around me, my entire life. And, until I got to see content from people who were describing their life that - so eerily, and distinctly - described my own (in ways that I had been -- long hiding), I finally began to peel back the countless scabbed over layers of autist masking that I had to put up.

I don't think that non-autistic people can really understand the level of micromanagement anyone who is, and can, undergoes. And it's much more complex when you're also queer, and a millennial raised into an age where you're not allowed to be any of those things. You were actively shamed for them. (It goes without saying that, obviously, any level of racialization increases that duress. And, of course, I can't speak to that firsthand. But there's plenty of great content creators out there that talk about that at length, nowadays.)

Which is to say, that I -- quite literally -- wasn't allowing myself, mentally or physically, to move.

After a lifetime of having to freeze all movement, it was like being within a constant prison of my own warden-ing. And I never allowed myself to acknowledge the fact that I had internalized mental and physical restraints, from being in a world that stopped me moving in ways I naturally need to move, to regulate my nervous system. So, needless to say, I was on fucking edge, always.

Because I had been internalizing the self-hatred of all my natural inclinations. It went -- So Dar -- beyond the typical bullying that cringe culture inflicts upon everyone. It went So Far beyond any kind of hiding in a closet. My own body had become a fucking prison cell from my full sense of self, that I was never allowed to embrace. I was falsely imprisoned inside of my own body.

So, as I described extensively in the first volume, I acted like I hated myself because I did hate myself. I hated myself in ways that I couldn't have possibly articulated then. I was internalizing the systemic hatred that this society demands of autistic people. Word on the street is that not all of us go on to embody this pervasive sense of self-hatred. But, that it is, unfortunately, rare.

Which, again, is why our substance abuse is So common, and average autist life expectancy used to be 36, and is now 39. I'm a community elder at 33-years-old. This world would prefer me dead.

If readers have in fact read the first volume of this memoir series, y'all will see that one thing is abundantly clear: it is a miracle that I am alive.

Which is to say, if I wasn't given the space and, yeah, the extreme isolation that COVID started; If I was not kicked – entirely -- off my fucking bullshit into rock bottom during 2020, between the loss of my mother, and the loss of basically everything, living off of corporate blood money, I can guarantee that I would be dead right now.

Because I'd be still drinking at the levels that I was. I would still be blacking out, regularly, not recognizing that I am autistic. And, therefore, not able to meet or cope with any of my needs in healthy ways. I would be working myself to death and drinking to still throw up, profusely. I would be forgetting keys in the front door, leaving myself an open target to -- who the fuck knows who -- in my nightly blacked out state.

That first year opened the door to my realizing that I wasn't drinking because I just wanted to.

I was drinking because in public I needed to, to socially survive. And turns out, if I have, literally, any other coping mechanisms, I don't need that.

And that was actively killing me. As any kind of substance abuse is known to do. As was the entire mental and physical duress of my overwork, my unprocessed lifetime of sexual violence, lack of all basic care, and having to pretend to be who I am not, which triggered my fight or flight, almost constantly, as a PDA profile autistic. Because basic demands trigger my fight or flight, putting me into a state of constant stress -- beyond the likes of which -- a non-autistic (and, maybe, even a non-PDA) person couldn't possibly understand.

Imagine if you experienced a panic attack every day, multiple times a day, for the first 30 years of your life. Can you imagine how you might feel by the age of 30? Spoiler alert: it's **Bad**. It's an absolute misery that I wouldn't wish on anyone, besides, of course, pedophiles, rapists, and Nazis.

Lil' bird, It's Time to Wake Up (& Move)!

This is why, as soon as I started learning who I actually am, and why I had such an enormous difficulty with just surviving for the first three decades of my whole fucking life, as soon as I learned that I had any inkling of ability to care for myself, I was able to thrive amidst unprecedented global crises and uncertainties. A chaos state has been my bread and butter, my entire fucking life.

Which is to say, that there is a distinct difference between someone like me, and the non-autistic person who has never spent time in solitude, and openly says they can't possibly stand to be alone.

Not to say that I don't ever experience loneliness because, of course, I do. I'm still a human being.

But it is to say that the thing that has distinctly differentiated between my experience, as a late in life realized autistic person, and a non-autistic person who entered this pandemic is that: quite literally everything for the first 30 years of my life was horrific and miserable because I lived in a society that absolutely hates my fucking guts and has done everything it can to normalize the dehumanization of autists like me for living as ourselves. In other words, we're "the bad guy[s]".

And these and more systemic discriminations against autists are very / newly well-documented.

Might I remind readers of all the statistics that I listed at the end of my first memoir, in the start of chapter five. Those are just merely the beginning.

Again, we know that self-diagnosis is incredibly accurate. People need to recognize experiential criteria must amend the traditional observational diagnostic criteria that failed us. Pay attention to all the research from the last 10 to 15 years about autism. All of that research is what I learned, and started to really dig into, around 2020 and 2021.

I'm still by no means an expert on every way an autistic person can experience life because we're not a hive-mind. I can only speak to my own experience and the knowledge that I've gained about recent research on autists. And specifically, the countless lost generations of autists because of how badly the formal criteria fails most of us.

Which is to say, the likelihood of me having actually obtained a PhD, done the research that I did (after having survived the life that I had, that, really, in every instance, should have disqualified me from ever getting a PhD in the first place), has miraculously collided into my ability to see all these things together, in tandem, and how: we only know we know, everything becomes normal repetition, and that everything is connected. So...

As horrible as my life has been, my specific life is the perfect breeding ground, in many ways for people to understand the full torment of what it means to not know who you are as an autist, until the age of 30. Even on TikTok, I've never seen anyone describe all experience(s) that I've lived.

Despite the fact I know that I fall into most of the terrifying statistics, regarding our substance abuse and sexual violence that we experience at high rates compared to non-autistic people, I know only because of recent research. This new research changes everything. Again, I mention it in short in chapter 5 of the last book, for a reason.

(In this one, throughout the following chapters I expand more in depth on the final two shortest chapters of total first book's five. This volume is shorter than the first because I focus in depth on the self-realizations that I've made, while being almost entirely alone for the last four years.)

Which is to say, let me remind, as I did within my dissertation project, that besides access to social media platforms, the level of isolation I have endured is equivalent to the most inhumane form of psychological and physical torture one can sustain. Most of my last four years could be considered little more than solitary confinement.

For the vast majority of the last four years, I have been almost - entirely alone - in one apartment or another, connected safely only behind one screen or another, through social media platforms. And if I wasn't, I was around people who acted as if an ongoing cardiovascular disease doesn't exist.

They acted as if me taking precautions to prevent from contracting C19 as someone known high risk for long-COVID and, also, a severe case of COVID. This is normal systemic discrimination.

Within prison, the level of isolation that I have lived throughout the last four years is considered a form of corporal punishment that is deemed too inhumane to endure for more than a few months.

And yet, in hindsight, this is still ***The Most*** relaxed, my nervous system has been in my entire life. That's ***Really*** fucking saying something.

Disclosing an experience of extreme isolation during this era is a narrative that I haven't seen anyone else articulate in fullness, that I do herein.

Because most people don't pay attention to the most recent research, and thus are misled by the CDC into deep denial, to act like COVID-19 doesn't even exist anymore. This also includes most authors that I've seen writing about this era.

Most disappointingly, those who write about sex.

But, anyone who writes about COVID in the past tense right now is propagating eugenics rhetorics.

This mass normalized denial has exceptional consequences on people who don't have the privilege to be able to pretend it doesn't exist.

Meaning anyone who is immunosuppressed, immunocompromised, are already disabled in whatever other capacity, and/or they're non-disabled but also just recognize that — literally — anyone who contracts this cardiovascular disease enough times is not going to survive without a lifelong disability, and untimely death.

Meaning, realizing who I am and embracing me, alone, for the first time in my life, while being able to afford to live on blood money (therefore not having to work myself to death), and not being in constant fight or flight - despite isolation - has truly changed my life in profound ways.

(Mind you, most of us couldn't afford to have the same. Yet, mass self-realizations still occurred.)

For me, those circumstances were why I was able to write my diss. in 5 months. It's comparably easy for me to endure bad things, simultaneously, since I had my entire fucking life. I have a kind of autism that allows me to benefit from hyper-focus. That is, quintessentially, autistic. I live / experience monotropism, for better and worse.

(It's also why I was able to write the entire first volume of my memoir, that's 200 some pages long within a week's time. Because it was the easiest thing I'd ever written. I'm used to writing incredibly comprehensive and dense academic articles, and a dissertation. All of which, usually, require me to seek out dozens, if not hundreds, of citations and references of other people's works.

All the first volume of my memoir required of me mentally was to recount my lifetime that I mostly, for obvious reasons, didn't think about.

Before that, I just didn't remotely understand my own life because I didn't know who I was yet. [For anyone who does wants specific sources that extensively back up any/all claims, that I make in this book or anything I said in the first volume, I have cited them elsewhere on Academia.edu, where I put all of my published articles/chapters for free. Because I know that there shouldn't be any barriers between the public | knowledge.])

With some of my basic 2020 realizations now uncovered, let's unpack them. What does it mean if the system is so dead set on dehumanizing autists? What does it say about this system that it's decided all autists are a hivemind? What does it mean if this system refuses to acknowledge autist humanity? Even us newly realized autists?

Before our realizations, we flew under the radar being seen as "quirky" or "short-tempered" or "whatever other microaggression". Now knowing that, without a doubt, there are probably millions, if not billions, of us that have been missed because of the criteria failing most of us, we are a lot more normal than people used to believe. That means the concept of who is "normal" is wrong.

That *Other* Time I Had to Live with & Care for a Being That Could Kill Me

If all that wasn't enough, closing out 2020, I had Twinkle again. Remember, she'd been living with my parents for the prior 10 years; my cat child I pawned off onto my mother, like a grandkid. It was time for me to resume cat motherly duties. But remember, I'm still allergic to cats. And I have a history of severe, potentially deadly, allergies to Goddess knows what (?????).

Have you ever had to take care of anything that can kill you? That being that you impulsively adopted because it was so cute to teen you, that you couldn't bare without it. Then at the age of 30, the deadly reality hits and your mom dies.

Imagine not all of it could kill you, but you're allergic to its saliva. Imagine you haven't touched another being in months. And finally, there is a being, that could kill you, and you can also touch it, all from the comfort of your own home. (So, statistically, imagine like your average cisman that you don't have sex with, but who's saliva, can kill you.) Do you want to give that thing pets?

Imagine you are a human being that suffers, if you don't touch anyone awhile, and yet, because of a deadly virus, you were barely allowed to hug your mom when she was on hospice, for fear of giving her said virus that attacks the exact organ that her cancer metastasized from, and she, not long after, died. The being was her baby for the last 10 years. She'd been with the family her whole f'in life. She slept in your bed as a kitten.

She knows no one else. She's only about 11 years old. And the thing that can kill you, can live a number of years beyond that. This is the only family you have, living in the same state. You need the company, even if it can/could kill you.

You're used to spending a lot of time with things that could kill you. This is nothing new to you.

Occasionally the thing that can/could kill you scratches you on accident, and you have to immediately go into allergy fighting mode. Your body reacts violently to the cute thing that can kill you's scratches. Your hands break out if you pet the being much. You have to wash your hands every single time after you ever pet them. But they have nowhere else to go. You really do love them. They were cared for, very well, by your now dead mother. And they're your lil' baby one.

Now, the thing that can kill you, you need to take to the vet to get their nails trimmed, every few weeks. And as much as you like to pet it, when you do, there's a chance it will drool all over the place. You put up gates in front of your bedroom and bathroom, so that they can't get inside. You automate basically everything they need to live: food, water bowl, litter box. They're mostly chill.

You decide that the thing that can kill you gets its own thrown. It's basically a large thing-that-can-kill-you bed. You get the very cute thing that can kill you very nice food for it. You get it very nice treats. You hang out like an old couple sitting in separate chairs, watching whatever stuff on TV.

You never really enjoyed the company of other human beings, anyway. It was *Also* always very uncomfortable for you. This being who's saliva can kill you, does not talk. It is cute, and even though it's saliva can kill you, it understands your boundaries, and has good boundaries itself.

You really respect this about the being that can kill you. You're not so different, you and them.

People shit talk you both for just existing as you are, all the time. Some people just aren't thing-that-can-kill-you people, and others just aren't Dr. bird people. Honestly, it's fine ¯_(ツ)_/¯

It was bad enough that the old house made my nose bleed. My nose and eyes really couldn't handle also having her. So, after months of trying to avoid taking regular allergy pills every day (because most of them have dairy in them and I'm vegan [fuller story explained in volume one]), I found a non-dairy allergy pill that I could take. Then, we moved into a bougie apartment.

Chapter [Two-Zero-Two--] One.

My nose finally stopped bleeding, and I was far less miserable after we moved into a luxury apartment complex. I attempted to seek out an organization to get the last place tested for mold, but I found out getting air mold testing is Expensive and ***Almost Impossible***. Anyway, that new place made me remember what it was like growing up in a suburb. Everything so incredibly well manicured. So many lights that allegedly kept the crime away. The pool was full of salt.

I had never lived anywhere so unwelcoming. I mostly stayed in my own apartment unit. Around this time, I tried to get my asynchronous teaching exemption, so I wasn't putting my life at risk, and the admin denied it a week before the semester started after it was already put in place. So, I stepped down from my teaching associateship because my mom didn't win blood money for her spawn to be killed during a global pandemic due to corporatized education administrator's bullshit.

A week later, I joined the all-audio app Clubhouse to be on a panel about doing so. (Despite having six years teaching experience, I was still completely unconfident in using my voice then. And being on that app and having connections that helped me realize that I had stuff to say of value, that could contribute to the overall well-being, helped me become who I am to this day as a speaker. The connections I made there and the work I saw being done definitely changed my life, for better and some for worse.)

That Time I Embraced More Gypsy Shit

Shortly thereafter, I started teaching myself how to read tarot. I ripped all the pages full of sexual violences I'd survived out of my flower pressed pages journal and burned them in the Moonlight.

Almost every night as I was drifting off to sleep, I was absolutely plagued with the starts of poems about unrequited infatuations. It was like I needed to puke those words out of my mind holes. (Think: the scene where Ron Weasley magically puked out tons of slugs, except in my case it was my lives' past compulsory yearning cisheterosexuality that I centered around cismen).

To repeat -- AGAIN -- I was almost entirely alone, all of 2021. I did exactly the right amount of thinking, sobbing, somatic movement, and telling myself that I "didn't deserve that shit", and also "what I did deserve, but never got".

I wrote a lotta positive ass affirmations down, and said them to myself, day and night. I learned

how to protect my energy and set boundaries
when people didn't treat me how I deserved.

Most of my socializing in the year 2021 was done
entirely on Clubhouse. I met some people that
were cool. Others that were incredibly fucking
toxic and thrived off of shit talking anyone they
could ever possibly contact -- no matter what
medium they were talking through. As always,
this audio medium was for better and for worse.

I spent a lot of time practicing how to hone my
personal message and translate the academese
that I'd learned to speak to survive in academia,
back into something that was most intelligible,
eye-opening, and useful to the general public.

Clubhouse was an invaluable space for me to do
that. But it also showed me that sometimes, as a
PDA profile autist with hyperlexia and stilted
speech, I just can't put too much energy into
communicating a message to people who are
unwilling to fucking hear me -- no matter what.

As days progressed, there were also cool reading
rooms that some people I met on there would run.

I also would run some myself, although I've
never been very good at self-promotion. And so, I
would start mine impulsively (because my PDA
profile autist brain otherwise treated running
them as a demand, that I would majorly dread).

When I was on that app, I also finally started working through and practicing putting down personal boundaries in a way that I never had my whole life. One particular person (who thought very highly of themselves, and name dropped / outright bragged about knowing transphobic-comment-spewing Judy Singer in person (before she was outed for doing so, by other scholars, like Dr. Nick Walker) tried to manipulate me, and I stood up for myself. I told her "you don't get to talk to me like that". And I blocked her cruel ass.

Point being, people like her and most anyone I'd ever met in the last few years had no fucking idea what I'd lived, and so they often mischaracterized me. They only knew what they knew of me, who I had to become to survive became normal in repetition, and everything was connected.

I began to see that I was often treated like "the bad guy," yet I wasn't the Fucking *Bad Guy* now.

A few short months later, I pursued my greatest pastime: performing infatuation of a cisman who was emotionally unavailable. My new muse. This time, I'd only ever talked to them through voice.

But my compulsory cisheterosexuality bird ass, didn't care! I was totally loving the fact that they used a lot of puns and seemed to have a good head on their shoulders. Every once in a while,

they were a little bit sexual with the way they'd
say something, and I was like *I see you* 😊

Besides some pretty ok poems, this experience
showed me that my compulsory heterosexuality
knows no bounds. The performative aspect of
that experience had become so normal for me
that, even without seeing him, I performed my
part. A miraculously strange *envirusment* self-
discovery. (The tea: After months of talking to
him regularly, I found out he's married and
monogamous. Somehow -- it just never came up!
Such a coincidence! Every once in a long while, I
still talk to this voice infatuated, punny married
friend, but they've definitely distanced
themselves for understandable / obvious reasons.)

And for a good reason, if you think about it. I
mean, I had already been alone for two whole
years, at that point. People who haven't lived that
long alone -- can't even imagine it. Again, on one
hand, it's basically just solitary confinement. A
form of actual torture. In recent books like the
Lonely Hunter, and the *Lonely Century*, as well
as research by Tiffany Fields (work on the
damage of "touch hunger"), it's well known that
no touch has extreme detriments to our health.
(By then, I had touched almost no one for going
on two years. So, I had only endured half of what
I have, now. But again, my nervous system had
never been more relaxed. I was drinking less than
I ever had before in my life. I was drinking less

coffee and more water. I was exercising. I was still able to meet people and have actually really good thought-provoking conversations on apps.)

Envirusment Disconnection(s) Breakdown(s)

Moving to a different, but not disconnected question, what does it mean if a society that refuses to take basic safety measures for a deadly virus (that's now surging again, as I write this), which, if not dealt with, could actually wipe out our species even before the colonial-founded capitalist-funded climate crisis (that is flooding and setting fire to vast amounts of the world)...?

What does it mean if said current society is so unwilling to recognize the damage of the current structure / orientation, that it would rather the most of us stay dehumanized, until the point that the planet – literally -- kills us all off, instead of just recognizing, we can't continue to live this way, and that we all deserve better? Why are the last two things *SO* off-limits that people refuse to even accept the fact that they're happening now?

The long-COVID and COVID-19 denialism are as sickening, disabling, and deadly, as denying the incrementally worsening climate crisis. They are both products of environmental racisms and injustices. Research shows that those hit hardest by COVID-19, in the U.S., are those in redlined populations. And we can -- almost certainly --

presume that Indigenous folks (whose lands were stolen and ruined by colonizers, and then the U.S. government segregated into reservations) are too.

Because, as usual, most every worst harm hits all prevailingly disenfranchised groups, the hardest.

Now seeing with the utmost clarity that the "universal human subject" has always been a lie, how might we start reckoning with the deliberate, federal funding blockade of: comprehensive sex education, the global loneliness epidemic, the sex apocalypse, and the vastly uncriminalized sexual violences? All of these terrors, and countless other carceral system violences, are connected.

I describe these phenomena and more in critical media ecological work as the "mechanization of humans," that is flipping into the "humanization of objects". Over the course of hundreds of years, these inhumanities became business as usual.

Said otherwise, this colonial capitalist society treats the human body as a machine, as "normal".

It's the reason we are equated to our data. As if everything in our lives can be measured in simply numbers. And why data colonialism happens. It's the reason all the foundational discriminations are built into these systems (including, algorithms) as features of the ongoing inhumane *envirusment*.

Going back even farther, it's the reason why the autism criteria has failed so many of us. It's the reason why color-paved racisms were built into U.S. infrastructure by racist humans acting *as* racist media within society building processes.

Its why, for some, anti-intellectualism is valid and rational. For historically and intentionally targeted groups, anti-intellectualism is justified because Enlightenment authorities, throughout history have, and in the present continue to, lie[d] as if they're Objective / represent everyone, when they never have been, and they never do. Instead, they lie, disinform, and miseducate the most of us into hurting ourselves and others in confusion.

It's the same reason why the CDC has become reputationally bankrupt, choosing profit over all of our lives in this ongoing pandemic. It's the reason why people aren't masking anymore who used to claim that it was important to them.

Because, years ago, the CDC Director said that "it's really encouraging that 75% of people dying of COVID-19 already had four comorbidities."

It's the reason why COVID cases have stopped being tested for, and Biden ended the emergency order, stripping countless people of their only affordable form of health insurance. It's the reason why people can't afford to fucking live anymore. We can't afford any places to live because U.S. society prioritizes profit over care.

It's why for-profit prisons, the military industrial complex (which is the number one environmental terrorist), food deserts, and sacrifice zones exist.

It's why most millennials and Gen Z folks can't afford food, let alone, rent. And, why there's been a fuck ton of forever chemicals (PFAS) found in Thinx panties, as well as global fucking rainwater (that obviously goes into our drinking water, and anything else rainwater seeps into.)

It's why PFAS **Could** be cleaned out, but it's apparently "not profitable enough" to do so. So, global governance haven't prioritized it. It's why they use language of "sustainability" instead of "regeneration". Its why gardens are focused on instead of food forests. All because we only know what we know, everything has become normal in repetition, and everything is connected.

Envirusment Connection Breakthrough(s)

In other ways, I actually had not realized that I did need this long time alone. And I finally got what I needed, despite the unprecedented state of the world and everything going on in my personal and professional life that had me grieving and overworking to prepare for the awful job market.

At that time, the isolation felt like something basically everyone was taking part in. So, it made me feel less alone, knowing that everyone else was experiencing it in their own way. (Though, not everyone in the world was living entirely alone after their mom passed away from lung cancer.)

On August 21st, 2021, I published a piece in the online outlet *In Media Res: A Media Commons Project* that I called "That's Miss[ed] Diagnosis to You, Sir: Mediated Grieving Over the Neurodivergent Gender Gap". It was in their issue on Grieving, and I used it to detail ways that the universalized Enlightenment subject has "poisoned the waters" of our understanding about what autism and other neurotypes really are now.

(As you can see, at the time, around then I was still mistakenly using the words "neurodivergent" and "autistic" nearly interchangeably. I had only recently learned "neurodivergent" was a reductive binary opposite to neurotypical, and that it means many *Many* neurotypes, beyond autism or ADHD. I also did make note of that inside said essay, and linked to a source that did a pretty great job of detailing why this happened.)

About a month after that, I was interviewed in a piece in *Good Morning America* about the way that the design of mRNA vaccines was incredibly cisheterosexist because most all medical research is based around the white cismale medical body.

I was chosen primarily because, unfortunately, after my first Pfizer shot, the period I had later that month was the most painful one I'd ever had in my life, and I felt like I was going to pass out.

Some medical doctors in the piece admitted that due to biases within the medical industrial complex, and the authority gap this and more has led to inequities in medical design and treatment to occur as normal, and it was a serious problem. I already knew that as a critical media ecologist.

However, as often happens, the bit that the *GMA* reporter included in that article reduced my research description to totally decontextualized, almost vaccine-denial looking, empty opinion. (The authority gap definitely won that one 😔)

Anyway, back to my experience of 2021. As a person completely alone for two years, at that point, I spent time learning that *Far **Too Many*** other people were living in very ***Very*** abusive situations, and my research documented that. (And, yes, any amount is far too many.) My dissertation gave me an opportunity to look at what exactly was going on, in a very thorough way, as I was experiencing isolation. In many ways writing my dissertation gave me space to process things that I otherwise never would have, alongside writing a fuck ton of poetry to process all my past emotional, verbal, and sexual abuses.

It allowed me to realize that in many ways, it was actually a huge relief not to have the social burden of going out and potentially feeling socially pressured to flirt with, date, and/or eventually have sex with cismen. But it also put into perspective for me that I don't know if I'm ever going to trust anyone I ever meet again to actually go through the process of "caring enough about other people's lives to take basic fucking preventative measures to protect others lives".

I fear that that is something that is going to stick with me for the rest of my life: Seeing Just, how many people don't give a single fuck if other people die because they somehow think they're invincible, despite the fact, this thing can disable and kill basically anyone completely at random.

And after 1 million deaths in the US alone, I don't know how that wasn't made clear to folks.

I don't know how people couldn't possibly care about how serious this virus remains. No matter how much they're in denial, I can't understand.

I don't know if it's just because of the level of trauma that I've lived through all my life or what. I can't see an excuse for ignoring how serious both COVID-19 and the climate crisis are to us.

This was also the year I decided to impromptu publish eight mini chapbooks of poetry of some of my favorite poems. I also started submitting my poetry to various other outlets and got other publications. I did a **Fuck Ton** of service work I never got paid for. My long ass CV shows that I worked my *Absolute Fucking Ass* off. Once again, I had nothing in my life, but low pay work.

That One Time I Almost Suffocated Myself

On a different bodily note, during my spend-a-paloza, in the later part of 2020, I had bought a Peloton bike. So, I was exercising more than I ever had in my adult life. But after moving into a nice apartment, I thought that I could remain isolated there without any consequences. I barely ever opened my windows. And I had air purifiers.

Despite all my heavy exercising, and incredibly diligent isolation in said new luxury apartment, I began noticing that I was, for some reason, having trouble breathing inside, and getting a decent amount of heart palpitations that I ignored.

Whether that was because I needed to always have my bedroom door closed, so that Twinkle couldn't come inside my room because I needed one place in my apartment where she couldn't go (since, duh, I'm allergic to her) or what (?) I was rather confused, since I was in great shape again.

Instead of caring about my health or well-being, I started writing my dissertation month by month.

The prior year, I had joined TikTok (that one week that Trump threatened to get rid of it [in 2020] and only lurked. I began gathering my 428 TikTok videos from late 2020 through 2021, attempting to capture an algorithmic moment in time of AFAB sociosexual reality. Even while living in it, I knew that time was momentous. I just didn't have the language to articulate it yet.

My primary artifacts for my dissertation were biomimetic sex tech. ads from the brand Lora DiCarlo. But while preparing my prospectus for my dissertation, it occurred to me that I should contextualize them inside these TikTok videos.

Around that time of the pandemic, the TikTok user base had exploded. An app that used to be dismissed as a "young person's dance app," during early years of COVID was now for the first time suddenly being seen as a legitimate area of study. As someone that was in it, I experienced how much it was changing many people's lives.

Me included. I saw how the TikTok algorithm was able to detect, seemingly impossible characteristics of people and categorize them, unlike anything that had ever existed before.

But I was at a ("lowly") R2, so I knew I didn't have access to any sophisticated software to grab the meta-data of these videos. So, I did it all manually myself. I went through every single saved video, 428 videos for five days, from morning until night, searching for them, based off of mainly the characteristics of the creator and their tag. I grabbed all the data I could find and manually, input them into excel spreadsheets. A process I had never been shown how to do, and completely created myself, as one of the first researchers to ever do research on TikTok.

There's a really high likelihood, that what I did will never be replicated ever again. And I refuse to downplay the reality of my hard work. I worked hella hard to do what I accomplished.

In hindsight, my autistic hyperfocus enabled me to do it, and write my dissertation in five months' time. I wrote the first two chapters in the first month. Took the first three weeks off and wrote a chapter the last week of the next four months. I was a lucky one in my short under-funded program to have prepared for this since 2018.

Most people in my cohort had no idea what they're dissertation was going to be about until their prospectuses were written. I had three years on them, preparing my project. And two years funding by corporate blood money from my mom's lung cancer, giving me an immense privilege of not having to work, while taking care of myself and entirely writing in my fourth year.

(I am incredibly proud of my dissertation. Most PhDs joke that no one reads theirs, besides maybe some of your faculty committee, responsible for over-seeing the project and molding PhD candidates into scholars. As of right now, my dissertation has been read by almost 1350 people just on Academia.edu. And I'm proud of that. I also read it on my Clubhouse account for free.)

Back to air, the week after I finished / defended my dissertation, I started noticing that my very expensive air purifier had gotten *Very Loud*.

So, I decided to finally investigate it more.

That was when I noticed it had a couple fancy detectors detecting invisible shit in my air inside of it. Turns out the CO2 (carbon dioxide) and VOC (volatile organic chemical) levels were ***Fucking Atrocious***. For anyone that doesn't know, CO2 monitors the level of air circulation.

Whereas, VOCs are an ambiguous list of things, emitted in processes of plants and humans, heat, etc. some of which have recently been identified as carcinogens. Meaning if/when you breathe them in for prolonged periods of time, they increase your likelihood of getting many cancers.

That's when I learned, my apartment was full of poison and *Very* little air. Hence my lung / heart issues. I also had containers upon containers of volatile chemicals inside my two-bedroom unit, as well **As Many** containers of ammonia-ridden wet wipes and bottles of noxious hand sanitizer *As* my mom's cancer blood money could buy me.

The research about VOCs being linked to cancer, had only come out about a year prior. Whereas, CO2 levels are almost completely ignored, compared to carbon monoxide. Because, unless you do exactly what I did, it's mostly a nonissue.

In fact, that year, I learned that when you Google CO2 (carbon dioxide), the vast majority of search results on Google are going to mostly give you information about CO1 (carbon monoxide).

As most people know, carbon monoxide is very deadly in, relatively, small quantities. But if you don't have enough oxygen in a space over a long period of time that's also deadly. I was in a new apartment complex that had well-sealed walls. I was suffocating myself to death in my 2BR unit.

I know because, one night, I began to feel lightheaded and noticed Twinkle was also not feeling good, and so I called 911. The firefighters and building manager treated me like *Absolute Dog Shit*. Meanwhile, I didn't have health insurance. And I sure as fuck couldn't afford to go get my blood oxygen levels tested, despite blood money and feeling like I was imminently about to pass out from prolonged lack of oxygen.

I called them, and I walked outside to my car with Twinkle, experiencing confusion and delirium. They arrived and tested the space for CO1. A chemical I was not yet informed about. And in oxygen deprived delirium, didn't correct.

Most homes that have gas appliances have carbon monoxide detectors for that very reason. It's a chemical where if it's in your air it can kill you quickly without you realizing it is. But what I was experiencing, was an entirely new era issue.

I was living the consequences of someone who thought they could live, completely isolated, without opening themselves to the overall ecology. The irony of my belief as someone who does critical media ecological work is -- ***Just Staggering***. (But, I am just a human too, y'all!)

But, again, I only knew what I knew, then, everything I lived became normal in my repetition, and everything was connected.

So, I conducted more research. My mom always said that my grandma got bladder cancer from breathing in air fresheners. Guess what's in air fresheners, that causes cancer? Volatile organic chemicals (VOCs). And my mom died of lung cancer because of chemicals brought home on my dad's work clothes from BP Amoco. Guess what those chemicals almost certainly were classified as? The same motherfucking VOC chemicals.

If I didn't get smart, and fast, there was a very high likelihood that I would have suffered the same imminent fate as my own mother, and her mom before her. And, one day, I still might, from prolonged exposure to VOCs that are ignored.

Because in colonially-founded capitalist-funded societies, corporations can poison us and our loved ones for profit and settle for blood money.

Safe to say, I did a frantic house clean soon after.

I started opening my windows for at least five minutes a day, in the morning and night. But it was fucking winter. So, it was Fucking Freezing.

But I needed to air out the Goddess damned place to protect Twinkle and I's health and well-beings.

So that's what I did the entire rest of the time that I lived in that fucking air-vacuum-like apartment.

That Other Time I Almost Puked to Death

Despite all my new goofy fuckin health habits, diligence, and over a year of intense ass working out, one day, I ate either a) Red Robin (trying their vegan option for the first time in years) or b) an Alpha brand microwave burrito that ended up contaminated, and got incredibly **Incredibly** sick.

And I mean -- so fucking sick -- that I thought I was gonna die for about 5 or 6 days - completely bedridden. Only a couple months prior, I had defended my dissertation and became a Dr. But in March 2021, I woke up to the feeling I was gonna throw up -- everything I'd eaten *in my whole fucking life*. I had gotten food poisoning maybe once or twice like this in my life. But, honestly, I'd never felt sickness like this before.

Not long before this, I learned that Omicron can often times present like food poisoning. But I was living alone in my Dyson ass fucking luxury apartment, and didn't medically advocate for myself. So instead of doing anything, I was unable to move from bed for four or five days, clearing out my system, and hoping I didn't die.

I couldn't eat or drink for the first few days of it. Everything exiting my body was almost entirely yellow. A part of me wondered if I was detoxing from some sort of Volatile Organic Chemical overload in my body. But then, months later I also got an alert from Amazon that the burrito company, that I ate right before it was recalled. I even had it documented on MyFitnessPal app, so I had evidence that after documenting my food intake as normal for over a year, suddenly after eating their fucking burrito, I got that sickness.

I tried to seek out justice from that, but I never got a call back. I'd been vegan at that point for like a decade, and regardless of if it was contaminated with some sort of bacteria, or whether there was dairy in it, they very well might have fucking poisoned me (if that's what happened.) Truth be told, I'll probably never fucking know what actually happened to me.

The first few days, I could only get a sip of water. I brought a coconut water onto my bedside table. That and a little bit of actual water were the only things I could ingest for four days. I spent my time, mostly in a delirium, watching TikTok lives of people, speed running old-school Mario and/or scratching off lottery tickets. I learned just how unhinged TikTok live culture really is those days. I think that was also one of the first times I actually gave ASMR a shot. At first, I hated it.

All ASMR (even the kind I later grew to enjoy) made me deeply uncomfortable as someone who wasn't allowed the privilege of being embodied, and accepting any pleasure that was solely my own (This is why I wrote my forthcoming paper about ASMR intimacy in the COVID-19 era. To see a fuller picture of that, it's on Academia.edu).

Anyway, I had never felt so close to death before.

I think I actually accepted that I might die for a few days. And I was like, whatever, I finished my dissertation at least. I wouldn't doubt it if in some alternate reality, I did die. But, in this one, I'm existing, and I just haven't been the same since.

Luckily, Twinkle was living in the other room totally self-sufficient between all the automated things that were feeding her, giving her water, and allowing her to use the litter box, play, etc.

Anyway, eventually, I could ingest more fluids. And later still, actually eat some solid foods. Not too long after that, I tried to exercise. It worked for a little bit, but then I realized I absolutely couldn't fucking do that anymore. Like I said, I was in the best shape of my life for like over a year before that. I was lifting more than I ever had in my life and I had a fucking Peloton.

But ever since I got sick, I literally can't exercise at all. And I haven't been able to since. I don't know if I got food poisoned and it irreparably disabled me, or what. I don't know if I ended up getting Omicron and was just never tested because I was completely alone and I have long COVID. Or what (?) All I know is that based off of the research I've seen, autists are at high risk for long-COVID, and a severe case of COVID.

So, if it takes the rest of my life, I'm going to be masking and taking my health real seriously now.

Because for the first time in my whole fucking life, I actually want to live as who I am. It doesn't sway me if the rest of the entire fucking world doesn't mask. I'm not moved by peer pressure anymore. They can keep on continuing to deny that this cardiovascular disease doesn't exist, becoming more and more disabled and dying.

I had something to live for now, for the first time in my whole GODDESS DAMN life, at 33, and it was finally living as who I actually fucking am.

But what made matters then more complicated is, I had no job prospects and my lease would be up in June. During the last eight or so months prior, I had been frantically applying for academic jobs.

Two weeks before my lease was up I got an offer at Miami for a job I knew I was overqualified for. Because it was teaching classes that I had now taught since 2015: a basic public speaking course.

As excited as I was, I was incredible stressed about frantically rushing to find movers, and a place to live. The only seemingly livable place available that quickly was tiny student housing. I knew it would be shit and the outside looked like a literal prison, but it was a block from campus and my office building. So, I thought "fuck it".

Chapter [Two-Zero-Two--] Two.

It wasn't until after finishing my PhD, on exactly February 2, 2022, at 2 PM Eastern Standard Time, that I finally started reading disability studies work (beyond the precursor to autistic literature I'd mentioned before, that come out in the last 10 to 15 years). (I only remember the date because after I was impulsively called to read it, I looked and said look at all those twos that's really funny. What are the odds?! All of those fuckin twos!)

That day I started reading, Maxfield Sparrow's (new, then) edited collection *Spectrums: Autistic, transgender people in their own words* on the very first ever critical media ecology club on Clubhouse. That book changed my whole fucking life. A lot of autists reference Dr. Devon Price's *Unmasking Autism*, but for me as a neuroqueer enby, who at that time still didn't really openly self-diagnose, that book was my version of *UA*.

After that, I also read Yenn and Wenn's *Autistic trans guide to life*. These three books are hella groundbreaking, in that they describe the high likelihoods that autistic people are also gender fluid, two spirit, nonbinary, trans. etc. They clued

me into the fact that this is often totally normal
for us. They made my life of gender make sense.

If I can do that for any autist that has lived a life
of substance abuse and sexual violence that they
have kept hidden. I want to do it. So, here I am,
risking everything in two books, **Fuckin Doin it**.

After those books, I then read Marta Russell's
post-mortem edited collection (of choice works
during her lifetime) *Capitalism & Disability*.

Work like hers expanded my understanding of
the fact that capitalism create an underclass of
people, into the fact that the vast majority of
people who are on disability, can't afford to live.

It showed me that this underclass of people is
almost always disabled. It showed me that
anyone already multiply disenfranchised is most
likely to become disabled, so if you talk about
anyone that is the most disenfranchised you are
inherently talking about disabled people. Because
this society treats us all as expendable for profit.

By mid-2022, I was a newly titled Dr. bird, flying
to a new location in the Midwest. The summer
before starting my first post-PhD contract, I was
living on credit cards again. Blood money ran dry
after me living on it for two years in the terrible
U.S. economy. I knew my contract would start
two weeks into August, and I thought I was

gonna get a full-month's pay, so I got another credit card, living on it. This is the most forested and least polluted place I have ever lived. But between Northwest Indiana, Bowling Green, and here, that really **REALLY** isn't saying much.

All I know is that when I drive around here for 45 minutes it feels incredibly less soul sucking than even just a 10-minute drive where I spent my first 28 years. I had a fresh start. I thought $42,000 would afford me cost of living. *How naïve of me.*

(I thought, I would get paid 12 months. But I was in fact, paid only 9. I also didn't know until the summer of 2023 that 14% of my income was taken out over the course of the last year to put into a retirement account I cannot access until I quit. Meaning I was living on only $36,000. [Which is why, without generous mutual aid, I would be houseless during September 2023].)

The whole first year of my post-PhD work life is a blur of me always wearing N95s and black non-latex gloves inside my four classes of unmasked students, *who were **Almost Always** sick there* and/or absent from my classes. This was the very first time I had taught in person since COVID-19 had started. I was fortunate in that I was able to live off of gross corporate blood money. But, again, it was an absolutely disgusting and horrific privilege to obtain. My mom signed an NDA, so we could have it, but I didn't sign shit, so I've

shared a short list of some companies responsible
for poisoning my mom to death on the Internet
openly. Here it is again, right here! Exhibit A:

Exhibit A

A.W. Chesterton Company
Asarco, Inc.
Christy Firebrick
Eagle-Picher Industries, Inc.
Flintkote Supplemental Payment
Foster Wheeler 1st Installment (1/3)
General Electric Company
Grinnell Mechanical Products
Quigley Company, Inc.
Rust Engineering Co.
Sterling Fluid Systems
W.R. Grace Asbestos PI Trust
Warren Pumps, LLC
Westinghouse Corporation

Again, as I described in chapter 4 of the first
volume of this memoir, the paralegal made it
very clear to me that there are plenty more
companies who never actually pay a goddamn
thing out, despite the fact they poison our loved
ones for profit. Especially, folks like us who can't
afford to get a lawsuit -- will never see a single
penny, despite the fact, their loved ones have
been murdered by these fucking corporations.

It shouldn't go without saying that my family
hasn't been the same since my mom passed.
Some of my extended family have tried to invite
me to things like holidays to celebrate a God I
don't believe in. But each time they've gotten
canceled because COVID exists, no matter how
much they attempt to deny it at the beginning....

I haven't seen my dad since mom passed away. I
can't afford to travel to see him, and if I got
there, I wouldn't feel safe at all staying there. The
entire idea of going back feels awful / off-limits.
It's like when my mom died, so did my home.
And, as anyone who has read my first memoir
knows, I was never much of a *Family Guy*.

Since my mom passed, I only talked to my sister
because she's the one handling her settlement.

And then, recently, having that awful
conversation that I detailed at the end of my first
book. Which is to say, I basically don't have any
family to speak of once my dad dies. And he's
been in poor health, for a long time. Well before
my mom passed away. Sometimes he jokes that
he's going to die before the climate crisis hits. As
if me having to likely die through the climate
crisis in my lifetime is some kind of fucking joke.
On one hand it's funny. Another it's *Really **Not***.

Corporatized Education? More lk Crap Education.

Anyway, despite this and the constant risk to my fucking life, it was kind of nice teaching in person again. I actually genuinely really missed it. I forgot how much I love teaching in person. I forgot how much I like seeing other people in person. That's how long I was completely alone.

But by far the weirdest part is that I was now nearly the only one in my vicinity, taking protection of any of our lives seriously...?

Every single class I ever taught last year, I was made constantly aware of the fact that in those moments, every single moment I was standing in front of my classroom could potentially cause me to contract a cardiovascular disease that could further disable me the rest of my life and/or kill me. I thought that with gloves and an N95 on.

Most of my students the first semester were never masking. I knew this is because of the way the U.S. government and major health organizations had decidedly told people the prior summer that apparently "COVID-19 doesn't matter anymore".

So, there I was, risking my life to teach a class, I could teach with my eyes closed after eight years. And my students were - constantly - getting sick.

I became hyper aware of the way that their hands were placed on their desks, and then they touched their faces. The way their hands, touched classroom doorknobs and then food. How could they possibly not understand how big of a risk they were putting all of our lives -- every time -- they sat in a class around 20-some other people who are completely unmasked, after everything?

There were at least a few people out sick, almost every single day, throughout the entire semester. And none of them were ever wearing masks. I can't repeat this enough because it was actually tormenting. Somehow, they didn't math the math.

But of course, they only knew what they knew everything became normal in repetition, and everything was connected. So, because everyone around them was acting as if a sickening disabling and deadly pandemic didn't fucking exist or matter anymore, they all acted like seeing each other's unmasked smiles, making small talk in person, and having in person teaching was apparently more important than protecting vulnerable people fucking lives. It was "normal".

And they're college kids who want to go out drinking and do all the quintessentially college shit. If their parents don't take it seriously, how could they possibly take it seriously? They were at a point their lives where literally nothing seems

like it fucking matters. And, they're a part of a
generation that recognizes, better than probably
any generation before in our lifetime, that there's
a significant chance they won't live to see old age
because of climate change. So, in many ways, I
honestly can't blame them for not giving a fuck.
(But I still don't understand how they do it. I
don't know if my generation will live to see old
age fuckin' either with everything going on.)

The new deadly normal is also systemic because
other business-oriented humans acting *as* media
in society-building processes decided to profit
from them paying for in person university
classes. Those business-people have decided
money is more important than all of our lives.

Because of course, there are markets built around
students being in person inside university towns.

Entire real estate agencies that would go under if
they didn't move back into those college towns.
Because in many parts of the country, the main
economy for college towns is just that University.

So not only do local businesses in those areas
depend upon students physically coming back
into town and the classroom, so they can survive,
but there are countless other third-party industries
that have infiltrated higher education (as it has
become increasingly corporate over the course of
hundreds of years), selling students everything

from food to parking. Mechanized inhumanities of this don't start-stop at food bots. They extend into a professor dying in early years of COVID, only to have their university claim ownership of all their recorded lecture materials etc. going on to use and profit from their work post-mortem.

That One Time I Blew Up on TikTok

Speaking of technology, in November 2022, I assigned my first social media style speech in my classes. I decided to take my research into the classroom. That same week my first TikTok blew up. I decided to share a quiz that I made for married friend of mine, and then hundreds of thousands of people (formally Dx autists and late-in-life self-diagnosed autists) f'in loved it.

That was the very first TikTok post I'd ever made that so many people had seen and related with 🌻

It was absolutely overwhelming. I had no idea until that moment what it felt like to feel totally seen and accepted for being me. What I shared in the Dr. bird's autism quizzes were things I never told anyone before. Things that I was taught to be ashamed of for 32 years. Things people couldn't possibly have known about me because they were too busy seeing / treating me as "the bad guy".

(Last I checked, over 20,000 people thus far have taken all five quizzes I made [mostly the first one, to be honest]. And I've made raw autistic anti-colonial capitalist critical content ever since.)

I had already been a lurker on autistic TikTok for a number of years (alongside diss. preparation). But the algorithm was never nice enough to really show anyone what I was doing until that moment.

The solidarity hit me unlike anything ever had. I had never been more physically alone, or unsafe when physically near people, and yet, also felt so completely and totally algorithmic connected to a community I already had solidarity with silently.

Because I had never told anyone any of the things I put in that quiz. They were some secrets that had I privately kept from everyone for 30 years.

And tens of thousands of people resonated with my life. Experiences that the traditional criteria of autism ignored/s. (In favor of incredibly ableist, and historically eugenics-based, observed ones.)

My following there grew, and I shared more and more secrets that I kept from everyone I'd ever known. I watched others doing the same. I did as much research as I could get my hands on about *how*, and why millions upon millions of us had/ve been missed. I also experienced folks who have no idea what the fuck they're talking about try to invalidate our lifetimes of silent suffering.

The last two months of 2022, after I was finally
seen by anyone on TikTok (thanks, algorithm)
was indescribably incredible. Like truly I have
never been so accepted by so many people for
just being who I actually fucking am. And it's
because I know there are countless people who
are also amongst the lost generation of autists
who have lived their unique version of what I did.

It has never been made more apparent to me that
I am actually a part of something that is -- *So
Indescribably Enormous* -- so far beyond what I
could have ever possibly conceived, and yet we
all suffered in silence for untold amounts of time.
It makes me think everything I'd lived was worth
it.

On another hand, it was the most depressing
thing I could possibly reprocess in my life.
Thinking about the untold amount of us who have
gone to the grave never learning who the fuck
they actually are, and just suffering for their
entire lifetimes, until this one. It's one of the
biggest fucking tragedies, I can conceive of, to
this day. Because -- quite literally -- every single
other injustice throughout human history, can /
must now be understood differently, knowing
how common autists are. I can repeat that time,
and time, and time again that This Realization
Changes Everything. But truly think of – literally
-- any phenomena that has ever happened in
human history, that made a claim to universal

humanness in neurotype. Then realize that that was never actually fucking true. That thing is now different for the rest of human existence.

This changes -- *Fucking Everything* -- for better, and/or for worse. Because the more that I learned about research during 2022, and spoke with other people who knew a fuck ton more about autism and its multiplicities than I ever have, whether they were early diagnosis, or late diagnosed in one of the endless varieties of experience (that being an autist can manifest, like any other fucking life), I realized how much I didn't know.

But as you can guess, I also realized that the reason I didn't ever come to know it all is because I only knew what I knew, ableism became normal in repetition, and it's all connected to the overarching U.S. eugenics society, that never deemed autists as human beings. So, why the fuck would we have been seen as legitimate subjects for most of history...?

Of course, we weren't! And, of course, to this day so many eugenics logic consuming scientists continue to reinforce our dehumanizations. So many venture capitalists, also constantly fucking exploit our lives, as if we're bacteria to be cured.

Autists and autism aren't a fucking disease. We're vastly diverse human beings, who have a uniquely experience disability, and a neurotype.

All of our experiences are totally unique. None of us should be seen as less than human because we're fucking human beings. Why the actual fuck do I, or anyone else that is a late in life realized autist, need to say that? It's *So **Fucking Telling***.

Anyway, I considered revisiting almost all of my content and just rehashing it here, but, honestly, for you to understand the end of my 2022, it'd be easiest if you just actually went through all of my TikTok content from then, and watched what I realized, as I was realizing it, because it is quite literally in archive now of my own personal self-realization process, personally and professionally.

What's happening on #actuallyautistic TikTok has never happened before in human history, and it needs to be understood as a legitimate space of inquiry and knowledge creation that it fucking is.

Even though, yes, the TikTok app definitely has pervasive ass problems with censorship, terrible moderation, and the algorithms are almost -- all the time -- reinforcing every bias, built into every system, as features. The app is far from perfect.

The Problems That TikTok Is & "Solve"s

In fact, a lot of the time, especially in recent months, it has been reinforcing really horrific violences against many multiply disenfranchised people. That's obviously the worst part about it.

But one of the best parts is, it's also inspired/ing mass self-realizations that we cannot downplay.

It is both those things and much more. It is allowing so many of us, an untold amount of us, because of billions upon billions of data points that it gathers, to re-process our entire lives in ways that otherwise we -- quite literally -- odds are good -- never would have, in the same way.

Although, of course, yes, there were already self-realizations of many late in life realized autistic people happening elsewhere, before COVID hit.

However, the enormous extent to which the self-realizations were catalyzed by TikTok, and other algorithm platforms, really can't be undermine.

The sheer amount of data that the TikTok platform, specifically, gathers, compared to any other, has caused its algorithm to be unlike anything else, catalyzing these realizations in a way that is truly not comparable to any other.

And again, alongside the fact that the algorithm reinforces and centers almost always attractive by cisheteronormative standards white folks, it's sad to say, but this app is -- quite literally -- the best knowledge sharing device there's ever been despite all its egregious and fixable design flaws.

We can, and must, fix the algorithmic eugenics that are built into platforms like TikTok ASAP.

Especially, before some billionaire comes in and scoops it up and destroys it like Musk is doing to Twitter as I fucking type this sentence (8.22.23).

No matter if they destroy TikTok one day, or not, the changes it made are irreparably inclined here.

Again, the thing about media ecology, as a theory and approach, and why I love it so much (despite, its "Enlightenment subject" canon issue [like any academic subject]) is that it talks about the way that certain technologies *make differences that make a difference*. That means those changes last beyond any one technology becoming obsolete.

Meaning, the changes the TikTok has made to the global ecology cannot be undone. *For better or for worse*. And we can utilize that consciousness-raising because that's -- quite literally -- what these self-realizations are (not in a new age-y bullshit way, but in a literal recognition of who you fucking are for the first time in your whole goddamn life way) change everything about the way that we have seen ourselves and existed in the world. They change everything about the ways we relate to each other. And everything about the way that we exist within communities.

That's why I've been able to be both more isolated, physically, than I ever have before in my whole Goddess Damn life, and yet do still feel a better sense of community connection than ever before, because unlike what many people often say, the Internet is real fucking life. It has impact on our real fucking lives. This isn't some sort of nonexistent non-ecologically influencing space.

Everything that happens on platforms influences the way that we exist everywhere else in our lives, physically, digitally, and every other way.

Advertisers will claim that it doesn't (out of one side of their mouths), but then (out of the other side) they'll use platforms because they see the enormous power that they have to the likes of no other technologies ever have in human history.

That's also why the U.S. government wanted their increasingly fascists hands in TikTok too. And why the hashtag fascism has been made "so coincidentally" out of use, shortly after they did.

That's why I made that TikTok about how if they couldn't get into it, they were trying to get rid of it because it is such a massive change to the way that we can understand whether or not the system

is working for us. It's just one tool, but it's one of
the most massive tools to exist in human history.

And TikTok's should never be downplayed,
because the only people that usually make those
claims that it can't be a tool for organizing are the
ones who have a concerted stake in retaining the
current structure that is -- quite literally --
hurdling us all towards a climate apocalypse.

It's not a coincidence that the same billionaires
who are dead set on making sure the current
system continues because they are the ones who
mostly benefit from it existing, hoarding a vast
majority of our wealth, are buying these fucking
platforms. Meanwhile, most of us now can't
afford to fucking live in a house by the beginning
of the month or eat food by the end of the month.

It's the same reason the neoliberal transnational
capitalist class monopolized the mainstream
media since the 70s, and everything changed.
And, again, I say this as a media specialist / PhD.

This isn't just my uniformed personal fucking
opinion. This is incredibly well documented by
all types of media theorists. As well as
philosophers of technology, digital humanists,
and in my neck of the woods, media ecologists.

Dr. bird: A Queer Autist Elder is Speaking

For all intents and purposes, and to the known historical preference of Nazis (who said autists who don't conform to colonial capitalist logics and actions), I should be dead. But the systems didn't kill me. So now, I get to fucking live my fucking life as myself. And if me, sharing my experiences of suffering can help even a single fucking person, live another day instead of dying by the age of 39, it's worth all the risks I take.

As the months passed in 2022, unfortunately, I had to cut out more and more people out from that audio app Clubhouse because they began to be either far too emotionally overbearing, or openly discriminated against / belittled my experience as an autist. My lifetime that they had no fucking idea about. Again, many that I knew there thrived on groupthink / shit-talking people because they didn't have anything better to do.

Some of them were incredibly toxic to be around even a little bit, so when I cut them out, I was relieved. I had spent too much of my life for the first 30 years enabling people's bad behavior to want to be around more people that acted like them. I refuse to have my experiences belittled, as if I don't have an authority over my own life.

If there was a lesson from those people that year, it was that it doesn't matter what media you're speaking through, there will always be certain people who will try to tell you that they are the authority on who you fucking are. It's people who have no idea what the fuck you're talking about who treat you like you don't know what you're talking about. It's the people who are *bad people* that try to make others feel like "the bad guy". And those people can get fucking blocked.

Alongside anyone that belittles your trauma that they have no fucking idea about yet talk about as if they have all the idea of who someone really is.

On a brighter note, their mischaracterizations of me also further catalyzed me into starting to remember more of the many who's I've been. Their hating asses were why I remembered how much I was bullied growing up, to write book one about how the many "me"s were treated, terribly.

But also, how all the "me"s are queer and deeply desire a real and fulfilling relationship in person.

Because despite the fact I am late in life-realized autistic, who has strangely benefitted from my mom's lung cancer corporate blood money funded *envirusment* era isolation / algorithmic age connections on platforms like TikTok, I am still a Human **Fucking** Being, that has my needs.

Do you understand how long it's been since I've been able to be a silly lil' bird in private/public..?

As much as I appreciate my new healthy coping mechanisms and lifestyle, I also do miss having wackadoodle time, and any sense of novelty that I have not been afforded the last **Four** F'in Years.

I started remembering that in 2019 when I was talking with therapist about the fact that I am almost certainly autistic and they said "yeah, you fit all the criteria, but don't get a formal diagnosis cause it's gonna hurt you more than its gonna help you". They asked me once, what do I want?

And all I could think of was "a large wall-style bookcase (think like in Beauty and the Beast), and a smart, funny, and hot queer partner. I just don't wanna have to date cisman anymore ever again." And they were like "you know, you don't have to, right?" And I was like "oh fuck, let me just cry my fucking eyes out for a second..........."

Because it's felt like my whole life I couldn't not do that. But it's so fucked up to think about the fact that it's not like I'm not sexually attracted to them, it's just been a fucking nightmare to try to be with them sexually because of how this world is. Because of what they always get away with.

I remembered that I'd felt like I spent almost all of my life in every social interaction almost scouting out who I was going to be with soon.

I've dated so many men. Like, revisiting my life in the first memoir, I forgot just how many people I've had around me for most of my life.

It was like a game. A game that when I "won" I felt like I'd lost. Like a circus game where I'd won a big bear stuffed animal. Then it turned into an actual bear and then also wanted to have sex and I was like "what the fuck? I didn't want this."

In my dissertation, I wrote about the fact that I am almost certain that in this sickeningly violent *envirusment* era, any cisman who used to stealth (putting a condom on and taking it off during sex without telling the other person/people) would now do a similar thing regarding their masking measures to their "partners". I put that word in quotes because I've seen a lot of people go around using the term "partners," then not act like one in alleged monogamous relationships.

That year, I often wondered to myself if I would ever actually get to date anyone ever again, but especially, finally a queer person. I had before, but I mean in like a real long-lasting way.

I've seen more queer autistic people through my TikTok than I ever had before in my in person life. It's been the actual fucking best. They're all sharing things that are just so unspeakably relatable to me. As someone who has been around people for most of their life, but always felt completely alone, I was finally someone who was physically alone, and yet, had never felt more connected to any other community before.

That same year, I also finally put serious fucking revisions into my "Requirement Politics" piece. It had been prolonged from publication, even though I finished it in 2019, until, literally, this year (2023). It is now, in its final state. And better shape than it ever was. But I do wish that it wouldn't have taken so long to just cite things that should not been seen as "uncertain" but instead, common knowledge, at this point. Almost everything I say in it, I have first-hand experience living and/or pervasively happens.

It grounds a main argument in my dissertation, and chapter 2 of the first volume of his memoir.

It builds off of my first book chapter about the #metoo campaign, and the way it was co-opted by the Democratic Party. The ways that both U.S. parties are responsible for the revoking of Roe v. Wade. The way that both parties are responsible for the fact that the U.S. just recently overturned Affirmative Action. All this shit is connected.

And we see that now. We will not unsee it, again.

Chapter [Two-Zero-Two--] Three.

How does one describe the monotony of waking up for almost 1400 days, and during most of 'em, existing inside merely 800 square feet? There is -- no way -- I can describe years of this monotony.

Over the course of the last four years, personally and professionally (due to my research about sociosexual ecologies in this age), I have lost almost all hope in the ability to trust most health organizations and members of the public to take basic preventative measures to protect my health.

How is a lifelong sexual violence survivor and researcher of the sexually violent U.S. ecology supposed to trust any possible partner amidst this public refusing to take basic health protections?

Some may think I should have unsafely gone in public unmasked around countless people. People that have overtly accepted and act like disabled people's lives don't matter anymore. As if I don't know that autists (Dx or not) are high risk for C19 due to our Very Long list of comorbidities.

If not that, other minimizers may think that I should have just gone outside to enjoy the color-paved racist eyesores of late-stage capitalist suburbia. (Need I remind readers, I wrote my paper admonishing the deadening effect of U.S. infrastructure for both of these reasons and more. Please see that as my response to those falsities.)

Most folks nowadays completely deny that a contagious cardiovascular disease continues to sicken, disable, and kill us because the CDC recommended a deadly new normal. It has been clear for years now that eugenics is coming from inside the CDC. Hence, their director, claiming it was "encouraging that only those with four or more comorbidities were dying of COVID" then.

It was inexcusable and not even true at that time.

Unless you've lived this, I don't think you can ever really get it. I don't think you understand the fact that there is no end in sight for anyone that has experienced any level of disability. Or knows about the prolonged damage this virus does. The newest research goes to show that this is a cardiovascular disease that can cause heart, and overarching, harm, for upwards of years after the initial sickness. To ignore that is absurd. This *envirusment* reveals that the U.S. government doesn't give a single fuck about disabled people.

Since it began, this country has been ableist, and that bias bleeds into every institution. It's the same reason I wasn't introduced into disability scholarship throughout my entire PhD. Because neoliberalism doesn't give a single fuck about disabilities. That's also why the vast majority of discriminations mentioned today basically never fucking deal with disabilities to this day. And why institutions across the country have the nerve to claim COVID-19 is over, when it's not.

This is also why people ignore disability as if this ongoing pandemic that threatens, especially the most vulnerable people in our society, as if their lives don't fucking matter at all. As if all our lives don't matter. Because the CDC Director said our lives don't fucking matter. She said it's "really encouraging" that only we will die.

And then most folks literally ate it the fuck up.

They've chosen to eat inside a Chilis over all our lives. Now institutions shave away hybrid options, despite 2020 showing they're possible.

Despite the many people groups who require reasonable accommodations to protect their lives.

Despite the countless people who have died.

Despite the countless new people who are now formally diagnosed with one/multiple disabilities.

Despite the countless people who to this day remain undiagnosed, but still live and struggle every day, disabled because this system has failed them. Because this system is insufficient at best and dangerous at worst for most to get diagnoses.

The CDC sent the message that people "don't need to wear masks anymore," despite the fact the research at the time (that they cited!) said we still needed to, confusing the public into hurting themselves and others in confusion. They sparked organizations – nationwide – to stop testing and claimed that it means COVID-19 cases are down.

Their words inclined Biden to end the emergency order, kicking millions off of the only affordable health insurance, which ensured that COVID-19 fully fell into the category of a for profit health opportunity, and for eugenics to take new form here. In the U.S., this was all business as usual.

The CDC and any other disinformation and miseducation sources that claim COVID-19 is "nothing to worry about anymore" here, and globally, end countless AND uncounted lives.

They have, for the most part, gouged out and burned to a crisp our abilities to safely exist in most physical communities. Their miseducation of the public has destroyed the most vulnerable group's ability to safely exist in any third spaces.

Their messaging has generated endless discourses of animosity and pathologization of those who are nowadays taking basic preventive measures:

COVID conscious and/or disabled people -- for simply acknowledging and acting upon the reality of what's happened and continues happening.

The CDC's severely irresponsible messaging has made "safety at work" a thing of the pre-COVID-19 past for most people still forced into in person work, and for groups who are already the most systemically discriminated against, inside and outside of national workforces. Regardless of whatever intention they've claimed to have, their impact has catalyzed eugenics logics and COVID as an environmental racism and injustice issue.

They have exacerbated any and all loneliness crises, sexual violences, and nothing short of social death of those who are disenfranchised. Because all those violences are made worse and compounded with transmission of this virus.

The only other choice available for those who are most historically and intentionally targeted by most any and all organizations in this country, is to deny C19 too. Only to then, disproportionately, become sick, disabled, and die from this virus.

For this reason, countless people are currently choosing in person social death as one feasible alternative for the ongoing risk of physical harm.

This is not a lifestyle anyone should ever be forced to live. It is nothing short of a new form of home-based solitary confinement for the crime of choosing to protect ourselves in an era where the CDC decided our lives are expendable to profit.

And yet houselessness is also on the rise because countless millennials and Gen Z folks now often cannot afford to live in most shelters, due to rent price gouging and the existence of billionaires (the neoliberal transnational capitalist class). Those fuckers hoard wealth, hundreds, if not thousands of times beyond what they can spend in a single lifetime -- which they only even have because they take from the working masses labor (aka, mostly, those of us who also – literally -- can't afford to live in a house / eat right now).

Need I remind everyone, lack of physical touch has numerous harms to our mental and physical health. And, yet the CDC's rampant health disinformation and miseducation of the public has ensured our most vulnerable experience this.

This is the sentence that many continue to serve for simply existing in bodies deemed expendable.

Yet, this is the result of the CDC's messaging that has misled the public to believe COVID-19 "is not an ongoing danger to their body-minds".

Again, despite the fact that C19 has been found to completely destabilize people's ability to work in a country that doesn't pay anyone actually livable disability benefits, since that, apparently, isn't a priority in comparison to the military budget.

At this point, it should be blatantly clear that the CDC has repeatedly made deeply inhumane and irresponsible choices. We cannot accept their deadly message about this cardiovascular disease.

As I described in the previous chapter, citing other works, it's the same reason why redlined populations are disproportionally people who are not just Black and Brown, but also often disabled.

Because you can't talk about colonial capitalist environmental racisms and injustices without talking about the damage it does to folks' lives.

This is why we need to actively describe COVID-19 as an environmental racism / injustice issue. Because it *Fucking Is*. (A much more in-depth discussion of this is within my "Car as extension of whiteness paper: Not everyone's skin is extended equal", the first granted funded paper that I have published since finishing my PhD.)

Why Don't You Have Enough Money to Live, Despite All Your Work, Dr. bird?

Corporatized education is why I thought that I was going to be able to afford to live on $42,000 for a nine-month contract. It's why it was more than I ever made. It's why the state of Ohio takes

14% of my income and put it into a retirement account I can't access until this job is over (which means I'm only paid $36,000 to teach four college classes a semester). It's why I thought I would get paid out 12-months but turns out I was only paid out 9 without that made explicitly clear to me, leaving me to scramble to afford to live right now despite the fact I'll teach over a month before I get my first Fall paycheck of 2023).

If you read both of these volumes, it should be abundantly clear that I have done everything I possibly can to unlearn being *the bad guy*, only to still be hated by **Many** ableists as "the bad guy".

Ever since I regrew my PDA profile spine, that was ripped out of me at a rather young age, and social media has existed, I have assume the position of the the person with hot takes, that speaks directly. I know most people have no fucking idea what I've lived through. They have no idea what it's taken me to get to this point.

They have no idea how many times I should've died and how many times I wanted to end it all. They only see me now as some sort of outspoken "Know-it-all" "Who prolly grew up rich" and "has a PhD because they're Hella privileged".

That's not who I fucking am. That's not who I have ever been. Yes, I benefitted from the educational privilege of growing up in Munster, Indiana. But, I'm an autistic, non-binary, neuroqueer person that has struggled for basically everything they had, who had to rebuild myself from the fuckin bottom up. I grew up an emo kid, and had no idea who I was, for most of my life.

All I fuckin know is: No one should ever have to live like this, ever a-fucking-gain. I only realized that at the age of 32. No one should be treated like their life is expendable just because they're disabled. No one should be calling the lost generations who have suffered in untold lifetimes because some fucking assholes claims that our realizations of who we are is a fucking "trend".

Our lives aren't a *Fucking Trend*. But they have gone viral, because of how big of a problem the way that we've been failed truly is. Because we refuse to be silent anymore. Because we refuse to be all your fucking mirrors. Because you mock us regardless, of if we act like your mirrors or not.

Because we're not you and we never fucking will be, and there's nothing wrong with that. In fact, were Really Cool people who, often times, have lives that were made a living hell by our autism. So, most of us have endured a fuck ton of shit.

We have *Every Right* to be who we are in private and in public. And it's *Fucking Ridiculous* that – anyone -- at any point -- in their whole fucking life has been made to feel otherwise. And with everything I've seen, from my Dr. bird's eye view, I see exactly why it's fucking happened.

And I refused to have my legitimate authority be disrespected because of some bullshit fucking authority gap built to dehumanize the most of us.

I refuse to be disrespected just because I don't look like a traditional definition of a professional.

I refuse to be disrespected just because I don't look/write like the Enlightenment subject.

I refuse to be disrespected because I've been a sexual person and experienced an enormous amount of violence in a world that doesn't give a single fuck about whether I received pleasure.

I refuse to be ashamed of my pleasure. I refuse to be ashamed of having the body that I was born in, to no choice of my own. I refuse to be ashamed of keeping my body however, the fuck I want and calling it and myself whatever the Fuck -- I want.

My name is Dr. Bernadette "bird" Bowen. I am a nonbinary neuroqueer enby. My pronouns are (She/they/Dr.). I earned most of this fucking shit.

I shouldn't have ever had to fucking live what I had, or worked -- so fucking hard -- after having survived this fuckin world that wishes folks like me were dead. It nearly killed me -- ***Many Times***.

A world that continues to put all of our lives at fucking risk every single fucking day it reinforces colonial capitalisms. I refuse to pretend that that's not fucking happening, after everything that I've lived, and everything that I've learned. I know what I know. I see that the sickening, disabling, and death has become normal in repetition for most, and that all this ***Fucking Shit*** is connected.

No matter how much you deny that this has all happened / is happening doesn't change any of this. But we do have the power to change what happens in the future. And if we want to continue to live as a species, we ***Better*** *Fucking Get On It*.

Because right now we're in the middle of an ongoing loneliness crisis, taking place in the middle of a fucking eugenics context, that ensured everyone denies an ongoing contagious fucking cardiovascular disease, while billionaires and fascists destroy our ability to live our fucking lives and the climate crisis worsens more, daily.

How You Feeling After All This, Dr. bird?

Me? Well, as I said, last year, I moved my entire fucking life to pursue a professorship that doesn't pay me enough to live year-round. And I have absolutely no prospects of dating anyone safely in person. And I have no one to trust in the event any health emergency ever truly happens to me.

As I type this, I am living entirely on the support and mutual aid from my social media followers. People who may be reading this book right now.

Because this job, and most every other one that exists in this system, wants people like me dead. It wants people who aren't profitable to the current sickening, disabling, and deadly fucking system to become houseless, die of starvation, and/or the countless environmental catastrophes it so profitably orchestrates -- all over the globe.

The only cute being I can touch safely, could kill me. Can you even imagine what my life is like?

Please try. I really need someone to try to imagine, and to care so I can have faith in a future where I won't have to live this way.

For the first time in my life, I really want my Beauty and the Beast bookcase and the queer, smart, funny, and hot person to love. I want to be in a healthy fulfilling partnership with someone who likes me for who I have found myself to be.

I'm finally ready to be/do that now, but if the world doesn't change, I will never be able to.

A Dr. bird's eye view

On a different revelatory note, we have the ability to build societies that don't just sustain the current ecological terrorism that is happening. And we need to regenerate ecological symbiosis that colonial capitalism has thrown us out of, to the point that shit is like this. We can't continue to fucking live this way. I refuse to sugarcoat that shit. ***Disabled people's lives Fucking Matter too***.

I don't have all the answers, and no one person ever fucking could. But I sure as hell have a very comprehensive, and yet specialized, perspective regarding what has happened, what exactly is going on right now, and why it is fucking killing us. We all deserve better than what has happened, and continues to happen, every day. And we can build a future that respects all of our humanities.

If we want to live, to do so, we must listen to the most disenfranchised people who call for land back and a return to our ecological symbiosis.

And listen to activists who say that unorganized people can't just impulsively call for a #Gentralstrike without first organizing mutual aid and supply networks. As happens in this fucking system, without those integral life-sustain supports, the most disenfranchise folks are always going to be harmed the most. That's how colonial capitalism was designed, and on fucking purpose.

Don't police my fucking tone about it. Don't silence my honest fucking cusswords that I use to say this shit, repeatedly. All this shit is fucked up.

I am an authority on these topics. And none of the shit I say is hyperbole. Fucking look around.

So, what do we do now, Dr. bird? Listen to the most disenfranchised artists, activists, etc. in this society who must led us into creating a liberatory regenerative system. Start building mutual aid and supply networks. Drink some fucking water.

Do something nice for yourself. And never ***Ever*** forget the *Fucking **Facts*** that autism is not "just a trend" taking off on social media lately, and that we all deserve better than ***This*** *Fucking System*.